With love to our little angel, Zach
~ Mimi

THE WISE ANIMAL HANDBOOK

Kate B. Jerome

ARCADIA KIDS

Attempt new **skills** from **time** to **time.**

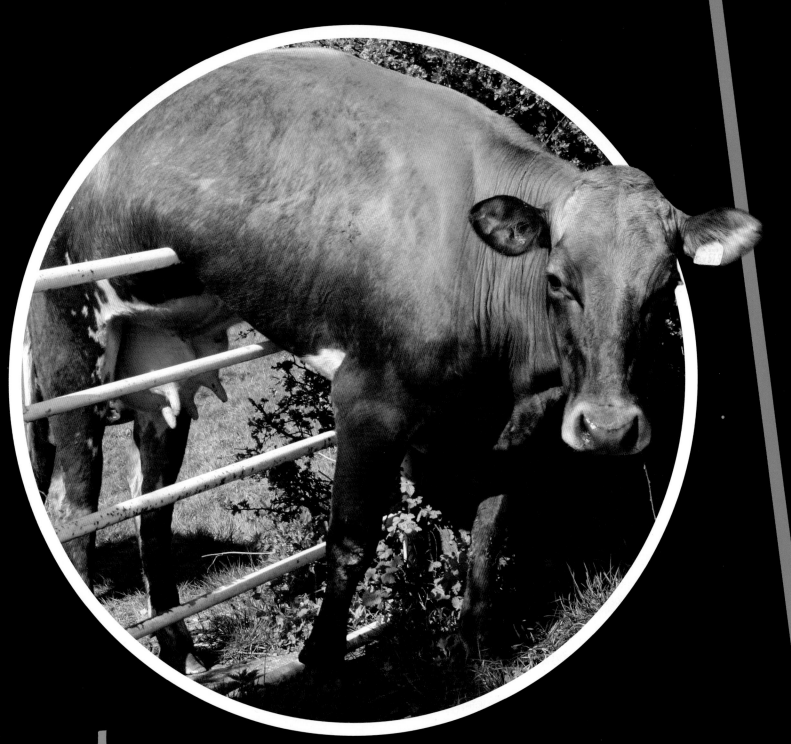

Just try to think them through.

And if you **find** you're left **behind**...

...then
change
your point
of view.

Try **not** to **think** of just **yourself.**

Invent new ways to **share.**

Stay close to friends whom you can trust.

But always be aware.

Avoid the tattle in the tale.

Insist that truth is best.

Embrace with pride the strengths you have.

Demand
to be
impressed.

Enjoy the peace that nature brings.

Ignore what's just for show.

Join **forces** when the road gets **rough.**

Admit
when you
don't know.

Remember **family** is the **best**.

Despite the ups and downs.

Don't **hide** from things that you must **face.**

Make
joyful
laughing
sounds.

Eat **healthy** food to **grow** up **strong.**

Be patient with your friends.

Try not to take a stubborn stand.

Be
quick
to make
amends.

Excuse yourself when manners slip.

Be helpful every day.

Keep trying even when it's hard.

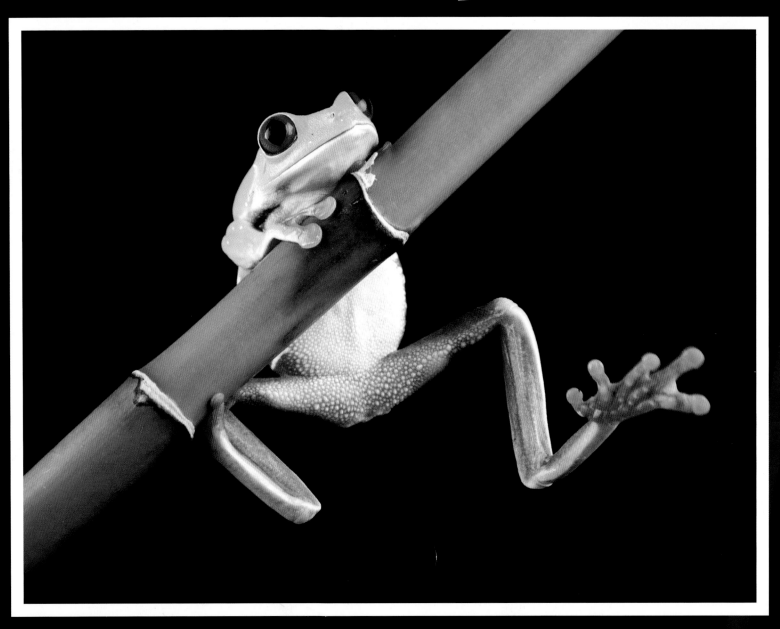

But don't forget to play!

And
sing

...and **dance** each **day!**

Written by Kate B. Jerome
Design and Production: Lumina Datamatics, Inc.
Coloring Illustrations: Tom Pounders
Research: Eric Nyquist

Cover Images: See back cover

Interior Images: 002 Anetapics/Shutterstock.com; 003 George Green/Shutterstock.com; 004 Sergey Uryadnikov/Shutterstock.com; 005 Gnomeandi/Shutterstock.com; 006 Bruce MacQueen/Shutterstock.com; 007 Henk Bentlage/Shutterstock.com; 008 M.M./Shutterstock.com; 009 Mikael Damkier/Shutterstock.com; 010 Brendan van Son/Shutterstock.com; 011 Michael Pettigrew/Shutterstock.com; 012 StevenRussellSmithPhotos/Shutterstock.com; 013 Pakhnyushchy/Shutterstock.com; 014 Patjo/Shutterstock.com; 015 Quinn Martin/Shutterstock.com; 016 Lincoln Rogers/Shutterstock.com; 017 Dirk Ercken/Shutterstock.com; 018 Karel Gallas/Shutterstock.com; 019 Orangecrush/Shutterstock.com; 020 Guenter-foto/Shutterstock.com; 021 Janecat/Shutterstock.com; 022 Shironina/Shutterstock.com; 023 Annette Shaff/Shutterstock.com; 024 Vitaly Titov/Shutterstock.com; 025 Rohappy/Shutterstock.com; 026 MattiaATH/Shutterstock.com; 027 Otsphoto/Shutterstock.com; 028 FikMik/Shutterstock.com; 029 Four Oaks/Shutterstock.com; 030 Ekaterina Kolomeets/Shutterstock.com; 031 Hugh Lansdown/Shutterstock.com.

Published by Arcadia Kids, a division of Arcadia Publishing and
The History Press, Charleston, SC

For all general information contact Arcadia Publishing at:
Telephone: 843-853-2070
Email: sales@arcadiapublishing.com

For Customer Service and Orders:
Toll Free: 1-888-313-2665
Visit us on the Internet at www.arcadiapublishing.com

Library of Congress Cataloging-in-Publication data is on file with the publisher.

Printed in China

Maryland State Insect

Baltimore Checkerspot Butterfly

Read Together

The Baltimore checkerspot was named the state insect in 1973. These butterflies are mostly seen in the western and central parts of Maryland. Have you ever spotted a checkerspot?

Maryland State Crustacean

Blue Crab

Read Together

The blue crab was named the state crustacean in 1989. Each year many people in Maryland go to festivals to celebrate their famous blue crab!

Maryland State **Bird**

Baltimore Oriole

Read Together

The Baltimore oriole was named the state bird in 1947. The male bird's black and orange-gold feathers are similar to colors found on the Calvert family shield. (The Calvert family founded the state!)

Maryland State Cat

Calico Cat

Read Together

The calico cat was named the state cat in 2001. Students at an elementary school in Allegany County suggested the calico because they thought the cat's colors would go well with the state flag.